Read & Respond

Ages
5–7

Read & Respond

Ages 5–7

Author: Sarah Snashall and Huw Thomas

Commissioning Editor: Rachel Mackinnon

Development Editor: Rachel Coombs

Assistant Editor: Caroline Carless

Series Designer: Anna Oliwa

Designer: Anna Oliwa

Illustrations: Mike Lacey, Beehive Illustration

Text © 2011 Sarah Snashall and Huw Thomas
© 2011 Scholastic Ltd

Designed using Adobe InDesign

Published by Scholastic Ltd,
Book End, Range Road, Witney,
Oxfordshire OX29 0YD
www.scholastic.co.uk

Printed by Bell & Bain
1 2 3 4 5 6 7 8 9   1 2 3 4 5 6 7 8 9 0

British Library Cataloguing-in-Publication Data
A catalogue record for this book is available from the British Library.

ISBN 978-1407-12629-6

Acknowledgements

The publishers gratefully acknowledge permission to reproduce the following copyright material: **Pamela Todd** for the use of text extracts, illustrations and the cover from *Whatever Next!* by Jill Murphy. Text and illustrations © 1983, Jill Murphy (1983, Macmillan Children's Books).
Every effort has been made to trace copyright holders for the works reproduced in this book, and the publishers apologise for any inadvertent omissions.

Whatever Next!

About the book

At its most basic level, *Whatever Next!* tells the story of a young bear's trip to the moon and back again – all before bath time! But the book is much more than this. *Whatever Next!* is built upon a child's capacity to imagine. At no point is there any indication that this adventure was make-believe. That bear went to the moon! (Jill Murphy revisits this theme in *On the Way Home*.)

The book provides a teasing story about fantasy and pretence which draws young readers into a quite sophisticated debate about narrative level. The essential question is: did the bear go to the moon? Any teacher reading the book to a class shouldn't question this, enabling children to read the book either as a straight story of a flying box, or as a story of a pretend game played by a little bear. This is enhanced by the way the central night sky scenes are fantastic, yet they are bookended by straightforward domestic scenes (which show Mrs Bear's lack of belief in Baby Bear's tale). As such, it can create some interesting discussions about stories and the nature of fiction.

About the author

Jill Murphy is an incredibly successful author, famous in particular for her *The Worst Witch* and *The Large Family* series. Jill started drawing at the age of two and writing at the age of six. She wrote and illustrated her first books at primary school. Her mother kept these first works and, of them, Jill says, 'You can see how my handwriting and drawing improved as time went by'. As a child, Jill was a keen reader, encouraged by her mother who was a librarian. Her favourite author was CS Lewis, but she also loved Enid Blyton and reading comics. She also enjoyed reading stories about boarding school and started writing *The Worst Witch* (a story about a boarding school for witches) while she was at school.

Jill went to a very strict secondary school where she claimed she could draw herself out of trouble. She also improved her work in other subjects, such as history, with her drawings. Jill left school at the age of 16 and went to the Chelsea and Croydon art schools. She tried to get *The Worst Witch* published, but, after being rejected by three major publishers, she decided to give up. She worked as a nanny and then in a children's home. Finally, she met a new publishing firm who published *The Worst Witch* in 1974 when she was 24. It was an enormous success and sold millions – and still sells well today.

Now able to devote herself to writing, Jill started writing and illustrating picture books, producing such classics as *Peace at Last* (1980) and *Five Minutes' Peace* (1986). Jill Murphy illustrates using coloured pencils; she mixes bright colour and soft tones. She often uses animal characters, such as the elephants in *The Large Family* and the bears from *Peace at Last* and *Whatever Next!*

Facts and figures
First published in 1983 by Macmillan Children's Books.
Won Nestlé Smarties Prize and Sheffield Children's Book Prize for *The Last Noo-Noo*.
The Worst Witch has been adapted twice for television and *The Large Family* stories were made into a TV series in 2006.

Guided reading

A first read

Look together at the double-page image at the very beginning of the book, showing Baby Bear coming out of the chimney. Ask the children what they think is going on in the picture. Encourage them to 'say what you see' even if it's as obvious as 'there are houses'. Draw out predictions and inferences about the cardboard box and where Baby Bear might be going. Ask: *Where do you think Baby Bear has come from? What is he in? What is he wearing?* Hopefully you will have a range of suggestions. Wait for someone to point out the owl and then ask the children what they think the owl is doing in the picture. Ask: *Does the image suggest friendship between Baby Bear and the owl?*

Move on to look at the title page with Baby Bear looking dirty. Can the children suggest any reasons why? Gather the children's thoughts about the story on a flip chart.

Read the story through for the first time. Afterwards, gather the children's first reactions on the board. Ask: *What were your favourite bits of the story? Do you want to go to the moon yourselves?* Don't lead the discussion, but capture any thoughts on whether he really went to the moon or not.

Getting ready

Talk to the children about pretending and make-believe. Ask: *What do you pretend to be and do?* Be careful not to suggest, at any point, that Baby Bear's trip to the moon was a pretence.

Re-read the opening of the story with the children (stop on the first double-page spread where Mrs Bear is looking out of the window). Re-read what Mrs Bear says. Remind the children about your discussion around the illustration of Baby Bear coming out of the chimney and their predictions about what he was doing. Referring to the reading of the whole book, can the children talk about what Baby Bear actually did? Challenge them to recall what Baby Bear's preparations were without looking ahead in

the book. As the children make suggestions, together try to verbally remember the list in order (rocket, helmet, boots, food). Once you think the list is complete, read the story to confirm his preparations. Can anyone suggest anything else that Baby Bear could have done to prepare?

This would be a good point to carry out the 'Make a box-rocket' activity on page 19.

Ask the children to pretend that they are Baby Bear's older brother or sister. Ask: *What would you say to your brother at the end?*

The journey

Read Baby Bear's journey to the moon from the moment he flies up chimney to the moment he returns (from *WHOOSH!* to *BUMP!*).

As you read each page, ask the children to suggest how Baby Bear is feeling and what he might be thinking at each stage. Ask: *Would it be scary to be so close to an aeroplane? Would it be miserable to get rained on?* Ask the children to work in pairs and take responsibility for one of the stages. Give each pair a large piece of paper on which to write what Baby Bear is thinking and feeling at their stage. Share the charts and ask the children to hold up their own charts and to get into the order of the story to create a 'feelings map' for the whole book.

Look at the spread in which Baby Bear meets the owl. Ask: *Do you think that Baby Bear would have enjoyed his journey to the moon as much without the owl?* Talk about friendships and discuss whether the children enjoy day trips more if they go with a friend. Look at the spread showing the owl and Baby Bear on the moon. Ask: *How would Baby Bear have felt on his own?* Can the children remember why the owl didn't like the moon? (There are no trees.)

Challenge the children to remember who else sees Baby Bear on his adventure. The passengers on the plane see Baby Bear out of the window. Improvise some of the things that the passengers might say to each other. ('Oh my goodness!'; 'What a wonderful rocket.'; 'Shouldn't he be in bed?'; 'That looks fun.'; 'I wonder where he's going.'; 'Help! That doesn't look safe!'; 'Am I dreaming?')

Return to the spread showing Baby Bear landing on the moon. With this page open, challenge the children to remember what happened before and after this page. (They might remember meeting the owl, but maybe not the aeroplane; they might remember the picnic, but maybe not the rain.) Now let them check in the book. Encourage the children to look at the pictures on each spread and say what they see.

Returning home

Read Baby Bear's return home. Discuss with the children where Mrs Bear was when he arrived. Ask: *What would you expect Mrs Bear's reaction to be?* (Cross about the mess? Relieved he's home? Excited to hear about his travels? She is as straightforward and matter of fact at the end as she is at the beginning.) Ask: *How do you think Baby Bear feels at the point of his arrival home?* (Glad to be back? Excited to have been on an adventure?) *What do you think he would want to tell his mother?*

Mrs Bear

Talk to the children about Mrs Bear's role in the story. Ask: *What do you think Mrs Bear thinks about Baby Bear's journey? Do you think that she really believes that he went to the moon?* Together, read what she said at the start, *It's bathtime. Anyway, you'd have to find a rocket…,* and look at how the two things she mentioned came to pass in the story.

Point out her encouraging comments – she gives practical advice in a matter-of-fact way. Ask: *Do you think that Mrs Bear thinks he will go to the moon? Do you think she believes him when he said that he did?* Discuss this with reference to the title. Why does she say *Whatever next?* Read together the line *You and your stories.* Compare this to her practical advice about needing a rocket. Temper this discussion with the fact that we actually see Baby Bear getting a rocket and going up the chimney.

Read the story out of order

Ask the children to tell you their favourite part of the story; find that page and read it. Ask other children to suggest pages to read – with the challenge that it can't be next to the page you've just read. With each favourite page read, ask the children to make a one-word note on a piece of paper. Model what such a note might be for the first extract ('moon' or 'owl' or 'plane'), but try not to suggest words for the other extracts. Gather in a number of the notes – perhaps as many as 20. Hopefully some of the notes will be different words for the same event – tape these ones together. Take the pile of notes and find different ways to put the slips in order. (In order through the story, backwards through the story, favourite parts (as voted for by the class) and any other orders that the children can suggest.) If you are carrying out the guided reading with a series of groups, keep all the labels and, as a class, compare the piles of notes and discuss any consensus and differences.

Finally, read the whole story aloud.

A starring role

Talk to the children about working in small groups to set up their favourite scene (or each scene in order) from the book so that they can film or photograph it. If you have cameras in school, each group could create a different scene from the book and photograph them. When all the scenes have been photographed, you can collate them to produce a class version of the book in photo form – or even an ebook on your interactive whiteboard. Ask the children from each group to retell the story in their own words, and once they have practised, record this as the audio for their book. If you have access to a video camera, use the same idea but ask the children to role play a scene from the book to create their own 'film clip'. Depending on time, you could use one scene from the book or recreate the whole story.

Each group could work on their own favourite spread to create several tableaux.

Once each group knows which spread or illustration they are working on, read the text, asking each group to listen carefully and to look really carefully at their illustration, remembering as many details as they can. Then let them start creating their tableaux.

For instance, if they choose the scene where Baby Bear and the owl have landed on the moon and are having a picnic, you will need some props, such as soft toys, some material, paper and paints. If you wanted to create small tableau, you could give each group a cardboard box to work inside, so they glue their backgrounds to the back of the cardboard box and then place the props inside it. Children can create their own backgrounds, such as the surface of the moon, using modelling clay, scrunched-up paper, or a piece of white/grey material carefully arranged. They could draw their own starry sky, by painting a large piece of paper in blue and sticking on sparkly stars.

Let the children photograph their tableau when it is finished. You can save the photo and show it on the interactive whiteboard, or simply print out each group's version. If you have time, you could ask the children to record their own 'voice-over' to accompany their version of the scene, using one child as narrator and different children to play Baby Bear, Mrs Bear and the owl. Or you could simply ask each group to tell their part of the story as you show it on the whiteboard.

Shared reading

Extract 1

● Before showing Extract 1 to the children, ask them to suggest what you need to do if you want to go to the moon. Create a list of the children's suggestions. Hopefully they will talk about clothing and food, but perhaps also learning how to fly a rocket.

● Display the extract and read it together. Choose children to come to the front of the class and circle the things Baby Bear did to prepare for his journey to the moon.

● Together, do simple physical actions that go with the text – pulling a box out of a cupboard, putting on a helmet, pulling on boots, putting things into the rocket. If available, use props to help with the actions (such as a colander for Baby Bear's helmet).

● Ask the children to suggest what else Baby Bear could have done. (Written a note for Mrs Bear, gone outside, checked the route, drawn a map, started the engine, talked to mission control.)

● Add these ideas as annotations around the displayed extract.

Extract 2

● Spend time recalling events from the story.

● Look together at Extract 2, without looking at the book, and read each of the pieces of speech.

● Ask the children to recall who said each line. Can they say how they know? Once everyone has had their say, check in the book.

● Once you've established who said each line, discuss what the character was feeling when he or she said the words. Ask the children to re-read each sentence trying to capture the character's feelings.

● Agree on the order in which the phrases occur in the book. Give the children individual copies of the extract to cut up and stick down in order on another piece of paper.

Extract 3

● Ask the children what they look forward to on a day out. List some of the features of a good outing.

● Discuss what Baby Bear and the owl might have liked to have found on the moon. Draw up a list.

● Ask: *Why might the owl want trees?*

● Ask: *How is Baby Bear feeling?* (Lonely, disappointed.) Talk about what they could do to improve their feelings. What do they do?

● Look at the picture and compare this with the text. Ask: *Are the owl and Baby Bear still feeling disappointed?* (Probably not – they look happier.) *Has the picnic cheered them up?*

● Ask the children to imagine that they are talking to the picture of the owl and Baby Bear. Ask: *What would you ask them about their trip and what answers do you think you would get?*

Extract 1

Baby Bear found a rocket in the cupboard under the stairs.

He found a space helmet on the draining board in the kitchen, and a pair of space boots on the mat by the front door.

He packed his teddy and some food for the journey and took off up the chimney …

… WHOOSH! out into the night.

Text and illustrations © 1983, Jill Murphy.

READ & RESPOND: Activities based on Whatever Next!

Extract 2

"Can I go to the moon?"

"No, you can't...It's bathtime. Anyway, you'd have to find a rocket first."

— ●●● —

"That's a smart rocket...Where are you off to?"

"The moon...Would you like to come too?"

— ●●● —

"It's a bit boring...Shall we have a picnic?"

"What a good idea".

— ●●● —

"Why, you look as if you've been up the chimney."

"As a matter of fact...I *have* been up the chimney. I found a rocket and went to visit the moon."

"You and your stories...Whatever next?"

Text © 1983, Jill Murphy.

Extract 3

"There's nobody here," said Baby Bear.

"There are no trees," said the owl.

"It's a bit boring," said Baby Bear.

"Shall we have a picnic?"

"What a good idea," said the owl.

Text and illustrations © 1983, Jill Murphy.

Plot, character and setting

To the moon

Objective: To make predictions showing an understanding of ideas, events and characters.
What you need: Photocopiable page 15, paper and glue.
Cross-curricular link: Geography.

What to do

● Tell the children that they're going to think about Baby Bear's journey to the moon. Ask them to turn to a partner and together try to remember the journey that he made.

● Hand out photocopiable page 15. Ask the children to cut up the page, organising the pictures into the journey elements of the story and then stick them in the order that they think is correct on a separate piece of paper. They should complete this task without looking at the book.

● Once they've finished and all the elements are stuck down, allow the children to check their order with the book. Get them to mark where their order was incorrect.

● As a class, discuss the most common mistakes that the children made. Did their order still make sense – that is, could the story have been written in that order or not? Talk about other elements that could happen in a different order, such as meeting the owl or having a picnic.

Differentiation
For older/more confident learners: Challenge the children to draw an imaginary additional scene for the story (for example, packing up on the moon) and add this to their ordered elements.
For younger/less confident learners: Provide the children with fewer images to order – perhaps only the first four or the first six as appropriate.

Good and not-so-good

Objective: To visualise and comment on events, characters and ideas, making imaginative links to their own experiences.
What you need: Copies of *Whatever Next!*
Cross-curricular link: Science.

What to do

● As a class, talk about the journeys that the children go on. (Going on holiday, going to the supermarket, going to visit a relative.) Talk about the good and not-so-good aspects of these journeys. (They can play a game in the car, they are given treats, they get bored, and so on.)

● Talk about something that the class has done together, such as a recent field trip, or even just going out into the playground. Draw two columns on the board headed 'Good' and 'Not-so-good' and list the things that the children liked and didn't like about the journey you've chosen. Some things might appear in both columns.

● Organise the children into groups of two or three and ask them to carry out the same activity from the point of view of Baby Bear and his journey to the moon.

● Tell them to draw the two columns on a piece of paper. What might he have thought was 'Good' and 'Not-so-good'? (For example, 'Good': meeting the owl, the picnic. 'Not-so-good': the moon is boring, the rain on the way back.)

● Use the pictures to expand the conversation with the class – did Baby Bear think the bump at the end of the journey was good or not-so-good?

Differentiation
For older/more confident learners: Encourage the children to discuss why the things they've put in the 'Not-so-good column' belong there.
For younger/less confident learners: Suggest to the children that they focus on one column only.

Plot, character and setting

Who said this?

Objective: To visualise and comment on events, characters and ideas, making imaginative links to their own experiences.
What you need: Photocopiable page 16, enlarged to A3.
Cross-curricular link: PHSE.

What to do
● Look together at the spread which shows Baby Bear finding the large box in the cupboard. What do the children think that he might be saying? (Possibly, 'This will do' or 'What a big box'.)
● Hand out photocopiable page 16 and explain that, in this activity, they are going to think who could have said the things in the speech bubbles. Agree together that, for example, Baby Bear could have said 'I've found one!' when he finds the cardboard box (rocket) in the cupboard.
● Ask the children to read each speech bubble, decide who might have said it and draw the character and write their name.

● Once the children have finished, discuss their answers as a class. Encourage the children to explain when the character might have said the words in each speech bubble. Can the children provide evidence from the text or the images for their answers?
● Hopefully the children will have chosen different characters for some of the speech bubbles (the last two bubbles lend themselves to more open answers) and you'll be able to compare the different evidence.

Differentiation
For older/more confident learners: Challenge the children to make up a couple of speech bubbles to challenge their classmates.
For younger/less confident learners: The first four speech bubbles are more closed than the others, therefore less confident learners could concentrate on these.

Characters

Objective: To visualise and comment on events, characters and ideas, making imaginative links to their own experiences.
What you need: Photocopiable page 17.
Cross-curricular link: History.

What to do
● Look together at the image of Baby Bear on the front cover of the book. Ask the children to suggest adjectives to describe Baby Bear. (For example, happy, brave, adventurous, and so on.)
● Ask the children to work in pairs and hand out photocopiable page 17 to each pair.
● Tell the children to cut out the adjectives and sort them into three piles, one for Baby Bear, one for Mrs Bear and one for the owl.
● The adjectives at the top of the page correspond to just one character; others could be appropriate for more than one character and the pairs will have to decide to whom they will allocate it. The

last three adjectives will need some explanation and discussion with the children before they are able to complete the activity.
● Forewarn the children that there is one adjective that doesn't belong to any character (horrible). Discuss how this says something about the story. (That the context for the story is a safe and loving environment – the only thing that can be described as 'horrible' in the story is the rain.)

Differentiation
For older/more confident learners: Challenge the children to add two words of their own to each character's pile.
For younger/less confident learners: The first nine adjectives have a more straightforward link to one character. Suggest that less confident learners focus on these words.

Plot, character and setting

What if...

> **Objective:** To engage with books through exploring and enacting interpretations.
> **What you need:** Writing materials and imagination.
> **Cross-curricular link:** History.

What to do

● Remember together the plot of *Whatever Next!* Talk to the children about the way each event leads to the next. (Mrs Bear suggests items that Baby Bear needs, he finds his rocket and other equipment, he's then able to fly up the chimney and get to the moon.)

● Challenge the children to think about how the story might have unfolded if the events were replaced with different ones. Taking each part of the plot, ask for suggestions as to what might have happened instead:

    ● Baby Bear wanted to go to the sea (instead of the moon).

● He met a dragon (not an owl).
● He couldn't find the moon.
● He forgot the picnic.
● His rocket couldn't get off the moon.

● Capture all the ideas on the board, reminding the children that these are individual changes to the story, not a plot itself.

● Tell the children to choose their favourite one or two changes (ensuring that the first change still allows for the second) and use these to write an alternative version of the story.

> **Differentiation**
> **For older/more confident learners:** Ask the children to devise their own story elements, or to write a comic strip to capture the plan they created.
> **For younger/less confident learners:** Ask the children to focus on just one of the story elements.

Baby Bear's expression

> **Objective:** To draw together ideas and information from across a whole text, using simple signposts in the text.
> **What you need:** Copies of *Whatever Next!*, packs of sticky notes, writing materials.
> **Cross-curricular link:** Art and design.

What to do

● Give each child a copy of *Whatever Next!* and a pack of sticky notes.

● Look together at the image on the cover. Ask: *What does the expression on Baby Bear's face tell you? How would you describe this expression?* (Full of anticipation? Happy? Not particularly surprised?)

● Ask the children to write their choice of description on one of the sticky notes and stick it to the cover of their book.

● Ask the children to go on to use the notes to stick a description for Baby Bear's expression on the following spreads:

● when he meets the owl (delighted, friendly, pleased);
● in the rain (worried, sad, homesick, lonely);
● arriving home with a bump (shocked, upset, surprised, hurt);
● in the bath (happy, telling his story, enthusiastic, talkative, excited).

● Ask the children to write 'owl', 'rain', 'bump', or 'bath' at the top of each note to avoid confusion.

● Once the children have finished, collect in the sticky notes and display them. Discuss the differences in the children's thoughts.

> **Differentiation**
> **For older/more confident learners:** Ask the children to also look at Baby Bear's expression when he's finding his helmet and boots and in the two pictures at the moon picnic.
> **For younger/less confident learners:** Ask the children to focus on the cover image and the image where Baby Bear falls back down the chimney.

Plot, character and setting

What they did

> **Objective:** To explore how particular words are used, including words and expressions with similar meanings.
> **What you need:** Copies of *Whatever Next!*, photocopiable page 18, scissors.
> **Cross-curricular link:** Drama.

What to do

● Ask the children to work in groups and hand out photocopiable page 18 to each group. Explain to them that the photocopiable sheet provides verbs from the book in the order that they appear in the story.

● Challenge the children to use the sheet to retell the story, with each child taking a verb in turn, going round the group until the story is completed. Tell them to help each other when they get stuck.

● Provide the groups with scissors to cut up the sheet into separate verbs. Tell them to shuffle the verbs. Can they now, working together, recreate the story order? Once they've finished, they can check their order with the book.

● Ask the children to use the verbs to write a simple version of the story. Reassure them that, apart from the words they've been given on the photocopiable sheet, they can use their own words to tell the story.

> **Differentiation**
> **For older/more confident learners:** Challenge the children to work on a polished retelling of the story without prompts.
> **For younger/less confident learners:** Provide the children with fewer words (*said, found, took off, landed, had, home went*).

Home and moon

> **Objective:** To recognise the main elements that shape different texts.
> **What you need:** Copies of *Whatever Next!*, large pieces of paper.
> **Cross-curricular link:** Geography.

What to do

● Discuss where Baby Bear went and what he did in each place. Ask: *Where was he happiest? Where was he accompanied by someone else? How well did he get on with this character?*

● Ask the children to think about the two main locations (home and the moon) and what happens in each place.

● Put the class into two groups. Ask the children on one side to suggest what Baby Bear would say if he was asked to talk about his home. Ask the children on the other side to suggest what Baby Bear would say about the moon.

● Give pairs of children a large piece of paper and tell them to fold it in half and then open it out again (to mark out two halves). Ask them to draw a picture of Baby Bear on both halves of the paper and to label one side 'Moon' and the other 'Home'. Ask them to annotate with words or pictures around each Baby Bear to show what he likes about the two locations. (For example, Moon: the owl, picnic; Home: hot bath, mum.)

● Return to the initial discussion about where Baby Bear is happiest. What do the children think now? Do the children think that he was happiest at home – but after he'd been to the moon? Or was he happiest in neither location, but as he zoomed out of the chimney?

> **Differentiation**
> **For older/more confident learners:** Ask the children to imagine how Baby Bear would feel in another location – perhaps on a pirate ship, in a spaceship or in a magical garden.
> **For younger/less confident learners:** Ask the children to focus on just one location – home or the moon.

To the moon

- Cut out the different elements of Baby Bear's journey and stick them onto another piece of paper in the correct order.

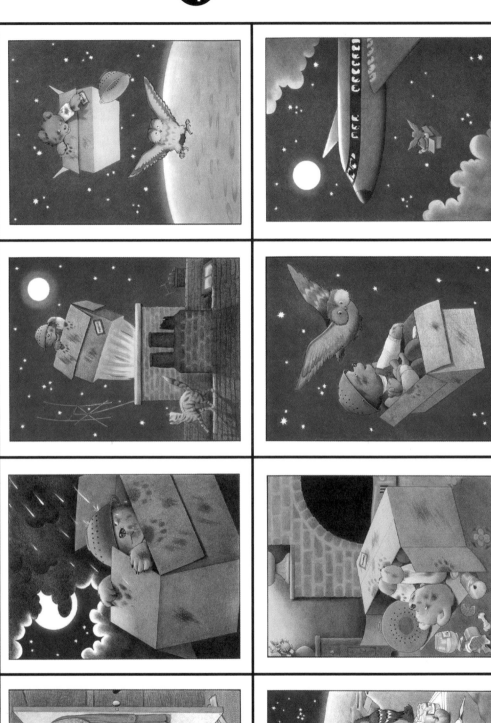

Illustrations © 1983, Jill Murphy.

Plot, character and setting

Who said this?

● Who could have said these things in the story? Draw a picture and write the name of the character most likely to have said each phrase.

Where's he gone?	Look out of the window. Is that what I think it is?
I'm getting wet.	I've found one!
Wow! Look at the view!	Where shall we go now?

READ RESPOND: Activities based on *Whatever Next!*

SECTION
4

Characters

● Sort these words into three piles according to which character they best describe: one for Baby Bear, one for Mrs Bear and one for the owl.

free	adventurous	patient
busy	kind	excited
friendly	happy	hungry
horrible	gentle	wise
messy	tidy	fast
imaginative	impressive	inquisitive

READ & RESPOND: Activities based on *Whatever Next!*

SECTION
4

What they did

● Use these verbs to retell the story of Baby Bear's trip to the moon with your group.

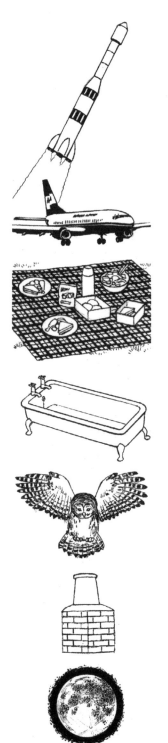

asked
said
found
packed
took off
flew
roared
waved
landed
had
off they went
dripped
home went
gasped
laughed

Talk about it

Can I...?

> **Objective:** To recognise the main elements that shape different texts.
> **What you need:** A copy of *Whatever Next!*, photocopiable page 22, scissors.
> **Cross-curricular link:** PSHE.

What to do

● Share the opening line, *"Can I go to the moon?" asked Baby Bear*, with the children and help them to understand that the whole story grows from that amazing first line.
● Ask the children to come up with as many 'Can I...?' questions as they can. Create a list and discuss together which of the questions could lead to an adventure.
● Organise the children to work in groups of three and provide each group with photocopiable page 22.
● Explain to the children that they need to use the photocopiable sheet to create as many

sentence starters as they can, making a note of the ones that sound most promising. Challenge them to come up with a number of completions for their favourite sentences.
● Give them time to discuss how each of these sentences could be the first words spoken in the story. What might happen?
● In pairs, ask the children to talk about how each of their stories might develop. They should work together to create an oral adventure of their own.

> **Differentiation**
> **For older/more confident learners:** Encourage the children to add their own modal verb, for example, 'Would you rather?'
> **For younger/less confident learners:** Let the children focus on creating 'Can I...?' (rather than 'Shall I...?') questions and discuss what stories these questions might start.

Make a box-rocket

> **Objective:** To explore familiar themes and characters through improvisation and role-play.
> **What you need:** Cardboard boxes (as large as possible), enough for one between two, paints and art materials.
> **Cross-curricular link:** Art and design.

What to do

● Ask the children to work in pairs and give each pair a cardboard box.
● Explain to the children that this is their rocket and they're going to use it to go to the moon.
● Provide access to paints and other art materials that can be used to create controls. Give the children time to paint their rocket, and to use the other materials to create control panels, levers, and so on for it.
● Leave them to discuss how the rocket works

and where they're going to go. Prompt by asking: *Who are you going to be? Yourselves? Baby Bear and the owl? Or another character of your choosing?*
● Remind them that they need to listen to each other and build on each other's suggestions.
● Allow plenty of time for the children to enjoy their imaginative play.
● Encourage the children to share their ideas with the class, then allow more time for imaginative play, incorporating any ideas from the class discussion that they liked the sound of.

> **Differentiation**
> **For older/more confident learners:** The children can go on to discuss instructions on how to fly the box.
> **For younger/less confident learners:** The children can decorate the box and make a smaller number of control buttons.

Talk about it

Chatting on a journey

> **Objective:** To draw together ideas and information from across a whole text, using simple signposts in the text.
> **What you need:** Copies of *Whatever Next!*
> **Cross-curricular link:** Geography.

What to do

● Look together at the image of Baby Bear first meeting the owl. Talk about the expressions on their faces – the owl looks surprised; Baby Bear looks delighted.

● Organise for the children to work in pairs and to improvise the conversations that Baby Bear and the owl have during their adventure. Encourage the children to start with their original meeting and then move on to their conversations as they journey to the moon, see the aeroplane, have their picnic and then say goodbye.

● Encourage the children to extend their conversation beyond what they are doing or going to do to discuss: *What are they looking forward to? What are they worried about?*

● Remind the children that this is a conversation and therefore they need to respond to each other. Explain that you will be listening out for them building on and responding to each other's talk. Model a conversation for them (For example, Baby Bear: 'Gosh! The moon looks a long way down.' The owl: 'I hope we don't crash.' Baby Bear: 'Don't worry, I'll use this lever to steer.')

● Bring out the rocket boxes that they have made and get the children to sit in their boxes and have their conversation.

> **Differentiation**
> **For older/more confident learners:** Encourage the children to polish their conversations and perform them for the class.
> **For younger/less confident learners:** Ask the children to focus on just one episode, for example, when Baby Bear and the owl meet or when they land on the moon, and to concentrate on two or three linked sentences.

Bath time

> **Objective:** To explore familiar themes and characters through improvisation and role play.
> **What you need:** Copies of *Whatever Next!*
> **Cross-curricular link:** History.

What to do

● Look together at the final picture of the story. (Baby Bear in the bath telling his mother about his journey.) Look together at the expression on his face. Can the children imagine the enthusiasm with which he is talking? Can they imagine what he is saying?

● Tell them that they are going to pretend to be Baby Bear recounting the tale of his journey to his mother.

● Ask the children to discuss in pairs how they will talk about going up the chimney. What will they say about the moon? What will they remember about the owl? Give the children

time to talk about what they could say and to make notes.

● When they're ready, get the children to take turns telling the story to their partner, practising it and feeding off each other's ideas. Provide resources for the children to use to record their story of their journey to the moon.

● Remind the children to use the first person for their tale. Let them change the story if they choose.

> **Differentiation**
> **For older/more confident learners:** Ask the children to take on the role of Mrs Bear and to challenge whether Baby Bear really did go to the moon.
> **For younger/less confident learners:** Encourage the children to think of the stages of the story and itemise five statements about Baby Bear's journey.

Talk about it

I think…

Objective: To listen to each other's views and preferences, agree the next steps to take and identify contributions by each group member.
What you need: Photocopiable page 23.
Cross-curricular link: Religious education.

What to do
● Ask the children to work in groups of four. Give each group photocopiable page 23 and set them to cutting out the discussion points and placing them face down on the table.
● Going round the group, ask them to take turns to pick up a discussion point, read it aloud and take the role of leader of the discussion, drawing out their classmates' ideas and challenging their responses by asking 'why?'. Listen out for the children picking up on each other's points and building and challenging them.

● Once they've discussed all the points, get the children to join forces with another group of four and compare their answers to those of the other group. Where did they think the same? Where did they think differently?
● Challenge the children to think of a discussion point to ask the rest of the group. Will Baby Bear continue to travel? Where will he go next? Will Mrs Bear join him on an adventure?

Differentiation
For older/more confident learners: Expect children to discuss, draw out and engage with their classmates' comments to a higher level.
For younger/less confident learners: Support the children as they give a straight answer to each discussion point and possibly say why they think that.

Where to go, what to take

Objective: To explore familiar themes and characters through improvisation and role play.
What you need: Copies of *Whatever Next!*, photocopiable page 24.
Cross-curricular link: Geography.

What to do
● Organise for the children to work in groups of four. Hand out photocopiable page 24.
● Ask the groups to look at the list of places they could go to on a journey. Ask them to agree on an order for the places on the photocopiable sheet, marking their favourite place as number one. Explain that they all need to agree on the order – and that you'll be listening out for their collaborative discussion.
● Next, they need to do the same with the list of useful items that they would take on their favourite journey, again marking the most useful as number one.

● When they've completed their lists, ask the groups to combine with another group and compare their answers. Ask: *Did the choice of journey influence the choice of items to take?*
● Give them thinking time to contemplate their journey and objects. Is the journey going to be easy? Do they lose any of their objects along the way? Ask them to turn to their talk partner to briefly describe what might happen on their journey.

Differentiation
For older/more confident learners: Challenge the children to add items to the list of things to take on the journey.
For younger/less confident learners: Ask the children to focus on putting only the journey destinations into order.

Talk about it

Can I...?

● Use one of the cards on the left and combine it with one of the cards on the right to make as many sentence starters as you can. Write out your favourite sentences at the bottom of the page.

Can I
Shall I

go
make
find
climb
explore
catch

SCHOLASTIC
www.scholastic.co.uk

READ & RESPOND: Activities based on *Whatever Next!*

Talk about it

I think...

● Cut out these discussion cards and put them face down on the table. Take turns to pick up a card and discuss the question on it with your group.

Did Baby Bear go to the moon or was it all a pretend game?	Should Baby Bear have told his mum he was going to the moon?
Did his mum know where he had gone?	Did his mum believe he went to the moon?
Was Baby Bear's journey a dangerous thing to do?	Could a cardboard box fly?
Would it be nice to go to the moon?	Would an owl be a good friend?

SECTION
5

Where to go, what to take

● Sort this list of places to go to on a journey into order according to how much you would like to go there. Write 1 next to the place you'd most like to go, and 6 next to the place you'd least like to go.

The bottom of the sea	
Desert	
Moon	
North Pole	
New York	
The top of a mountain	

● Now sort the list of items that you would need on your favourite journey from most useful to least useful.

Tent	
Map	
Torch	
Mobile phone	
Sandwiches	
Compass	
Water bottle	

Get writing

How to go to the moon

> **Objective:** To convey information and ideas in simple non-narrative forms.
> **What you need:** Copies of *Whatever Next!*, writing materials.
> **Cross-curricular link:** Science.

What to do

● Tell the children that they are going to be writing their own instructions for how to get to the moon.

● Talk about Baby Bear's planning. (How did he prepare? What did he take? Which way did he go?) On the board, make one-word notes for each stage for the children to use to structure their instructions (rocket, clothing, food, take-off, journey, landing, picnic, take-off, landing). Ask the children to note down these stages, leaving plenty of room around each word.

● Tell the children to put their copies of *Whatever Next!* aside and to get out their imaginations. Ask them to annotate each of the words with their own ideas for the journey. (Where are they going to find their rocket? What clothes and food do they need to take? Can they think of extra stages to add to the instructions? Perhaps some safety checks – is there a fire lit in the fireplace?) Give the thumbs up to any major variations (for example, the child who plans to trampoline to the moon rather than fly).

● When ready, ask the children to write their instructions, remembering to use imperative verbs.

> **Differentiation**
> **For older/more confident learners:** Encourage the children to be creative in their instructions, changing them where they can think of better or amusing alternatives. Challenge them to think what they need to do to ensure they don't miss the moon.
> **For younger/less confident learners:** Encourage the children to focus on writing clear instructions using Baby Bear's experience as the basis for their writing.

Moon journey

> **Objective:** To draw on knowledge and experience of texts in deciding and planning what and how to write.
> **What you need:** Photocopiable page 28, scissors, large pieces of paper and glue.
> **Cross-curricular link:** Drama.

What to do

● It's the children's turn to go to the moon. Get the children's rocket boxes out again and give them some time to pretend that they're on a trip to the moon in their rocket with a friend.

● Once they've had enough time to fly to the moon and back, hand out photocopiable page 28 and scissors, glue and paper.

● Explain that the cards on the photocopiable sheet include the elements from Baby Bear's trip to the moon, along with some new elements. Ask the children to cut out any elements they want to use and stick them on their big piece of paper to create a story map for a moon journey of their own. They shouldn't use all the elements but they do need to make sure that their story makes sense and that they remember to take off and land.

● Encourage the children to add any elements from their own rocket box adventure into the story map.

● Once they have finished their story map, encourage them to tell one part of the story to a partner and then try to write a different part of the story – perhaps the point where they land on the moon itself.

> **Differentiation**
> **For older/more confident learners:** Ask the children to think through issues they may encounter, for example, not having any air to breathe.
> **For younger/less confident learners:** Ask the children to focus on one portion of the trip, for example, being on the moon itself.

Get writing

Captain's log

> **Objective:** To draw on knowledge and experience of texts in deciding and planning what and how to write.
> **What you need:** Copies of *Whatever Next!*, writing materials.
> **Cross-curricular link:** History.

What to do

● Talk to the children about what they know about diaries, why we write them and who might read them. Explain that a log is a public form of a diary: a record of events kept by the captain of a ship during the ship's voyage. Ask them to imagine that Baby Bear had kept a log for his journey and written it at different times.

● Organise the children to work in groups of three. Ask each group to think of three points at which Baby Bear might have taken time to record events (for example, while flying, while on the moon, once he's home) and then to organise themselves to write one of the log entries each. Encourage them to think about how he would have been feeling at the point they are writing. Talk about how Baby Bear's feelings might change over time – excited at the beginning, but perhaps nervous; disappointed about the moon; miserable when it rains, and so on.

● Ensure that the children have access to copies of *Whatever Next!* and suggest that they look at the expressions on Baby Bear's face for inspiration.

● Once the logs are finished, display each group's as a triptych.

> **Differentiation**
> **For older/more confident learners:** Challenge the children to write a second log and to capture the formal style of a captain's log.
> **For younger/less confident learners:** Ask the children to focus on writing one sentence only for their log.

Pretending to be

> **Objective:** To use planning to establish clear sections for writing.
> **What you need:** Photocopiable page 29, enlarged to A3, writing materials.
> **Cross-curricular links:** Art and design, design and technology.

What to do

● Talk about the characters that the children like to pretend to be: pirates, fairies, princesses, and so on.

● Hand out photocopiable page 29 and ask the children to use the sheet to develop their thoughts about a character they might like to be for an adventure.

● The photocopiable sheet is written in a report format to help the children focus on the character type they have chosen. The children will enjoy writing labels for the kit they might be wearing (cutlass, fairy wings) and this will, hopefully, give them items to bring into their story.

● Once the children have had fun putting details onto their photocopiable sheet, tell them it's time to start planning a story that includes the elements from their planner. When will they use their cutlass or fairy dust?

● Provide the children with a simple structure to follow so that they can concentrate on their character: their character sets out on an adventure (think about what the adventure is and what they have with them); they meet someone/something along the way (remembering what they like and don't like); they come back (how?).

> **Differentiation**
> **For older/more confident learners:** Encourage the children to create additional character attributes, such as smell, favourite saying. Can they create a villain on another page? Give them time to complete their planner and write up their story.
> **For younger/less confident learners:** The children can complete fewer boxes on the planner.

Get writing

Journey plan

> **Objective:** To write chronological and non-chronological texts using simple structures.
> **What you need:** Photocopiable page 30.
> **Cross-curricular link:** Geography.

What to do

● Baby Bear's trip to the moon is a gentle adventure. Suggest to the children that they might like to create their own journey that doesn't go as smoothly.

● Hand out photocopiable page 30 to the children. Encourage them to fill in their planner with the ending in mind. Can they think how each element they add to their plan might make the adventure more exciting?

● Remind them that in journey stories, although the destination should be clear, it's the adventures that the children can have on the way that keeps the reader involved.

● Can they think of hazards to include along the way? Can they match the hazard they have chosen with what they might take or who they are or who they are with? (For example, a river of fire is less of a problem if you are with a giant eagle or a brilliant tightrope walker who takes you on their shoulders.)

● Encourage the children to use an adjective in each of the spaces.

● Once the children have completed their planning sheet, ask them to talk to their partner about their story plans before finally telling, then writing, the story.

> **Differentiation**
> **For older/more confident learners:** Encourage the children to plan a story in chapters.
> **For younger/less confident learners:** Where necessary, limit the number of hazards to one or two as appropriate.

Postcards from

> **Objective:** To draw on knowledge and experience of texts in deciding and planning what and how to write.
> **What you need:** A selection of holiday postcards.
> **Cross-curricular link:** Art and design.

What to do

● Ask the children to bring in postcards and bring in some of your own. Spend some time looking at them and talking about their features.

● Together, compose a postcard that Baby Bear might write to his mother from the moon. Ask: *What might it say?* (Perhaps, 'You'll never believe it, Mummy, but I'm on the moon. It's a bit cold and boring but I've had great fun travelling here. I've met an owl and surprised people on an aeroplane. Love Baby Bear'.) Capture the ideas and model the writing process.

● Ask the children to write postcards from other destinations. Can they write a postcard from the main character in the adventure journey story they planned before?

● Remind the children that they need to give the reader some idea of what it's like where they are and what they're doing there.

● Encourage them to think of the person they're writing to. Ask: *What would he or she think about the destination if they were there? What would they find interesting?*

● Remind the children to write in the first person and to say as much as they can in as few words as they can. Let them have fun with the address and stamp.

> **Differentiation**
> **For older/more confident learners:** Stretch these children to write an imaginative postcard from a made-up destination.
> **For younger/less confident learners:** Help some children with their writing by focusing on what they think of their destination.

Moon journey

● Cut out the cards below and use some of these elements to make a story map of your journey to the moon.

Fly past an aeroplane	Have a picnic
Land on the moon	Make a spaceship
Return home	See birds flying past
Take off from Earth	Take off from the moon
Learn to fly the spaceship	Find something special
Get lost in a cloud	Fly to the other side of the moon
Do some moonwalking	Meet some moon creatures

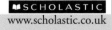

Pretending to be

● Think about a character you might like to be for an adventure.
Complete the planner below with information about your character.

I'm pretending to be	
What will you be like?	**What I will look like:** Draw yourself as your new character and label the accessories you are wearing.
Where will you go?	
What will you do?	
Who will you meet?	
What sort of things will you say?	
What do you like? What don't you like?	
Can you think of some things that could happen to you?	

Get writing

Journey plan

● Answer these questions to help you plan your journey story. Use an adjective in each of your answers.

Where am I going? _____

_____

Who am I going with? _____

_____

What will I take? _____

_____

_____

How will I get there? _____

_____

_____

What could happen on the way? _____

_____

_____

_____

_____

_____

_____

Assessment

Assessment advice

Whatever Next! is a book that can be quickly read, and then discussed and re-read many times afterwards. It presents a superbly crafted narrative arc in which events arise and are resolved and, as such, provides a great opportunity to assess children's developing engagement with the structure of a story.

After finishing a unit on *Whatever Next!* you should assess the following:
- Are the children able to recall the narrative order of the story?
- Do the children understand how a plot works (how one thing leads to another)?

- Are the children able to see how the settings passed through on a journey contribute to the story?
- Can the children see the narrative arc of the story? Can they see how the story moves from the desire to go on an amazing journey through rain to homecoming – there's no place like home…
- Are the children able to discuss the connection between the character and the story events? Use photocopiable page 32 to assess the children's grasp of this aspect.

What Baby Bear thought

Assessment focus: To use *Whatever Next!* to provide evidence of the children's understanding of the link between events and character.
What you need: Photocopiable page 32.

What to do
- Focus together on the first image in the story (Baby Bear looking out of the window). Ask the children for ideas as to what Baby Bear might be thinking and feeling. Encourage the children to think of as many ideas as possible. (He feels bored, he wants to have an adventure, he's thinking how beautiful the moon is, he wonders how far away the moon is, he thinks the night is exciting, he doesn't want to have a bath, and so on.) Talk to the children about how Baby Bear might be thinking and feeling a number of things at the same time.
- Talk about what they know about Baby Bear (he's resourceful, he's brave, he's interested in his surroundings, and so on) and how this might change their answers. Hand out photocopiable page 32 and ask the children to fill in what Baby Bear is thinking and feeling at each of these points.
  - Ask the children to think about how they would feel in the same situation – do they think that Baby Bear would feel the same things?
  - Remind them to refer to the illustrations to see Baby Bear's expressions.

What Baby Bear thought

- Fill in the thought bubbles to say what Baby Bear thought at each point in the story.

1. He wanted to go to the moon.

2. He was building his rocket.

3. He blasted out of the chimney.

4. He had a picnic on the moon.

5. He was flying through rain.

6. He landed at home.

Illustration © 1983, Jill Murphy.